Homework – Chapter 31
Reading pages: 211 215
Problems #2, #3, #12, #15, #18,
#22-26   *Due Wednesday

*** Extra Credit ***
Calculate the trajectory of a
rocket (A) travelling to
the M_____ (B) by the
mo___ ____ route
__e.
at _____
600
_0 miles per hour

See p. ___ ____ additional information.

Example 2
graph the following.

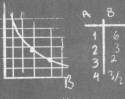
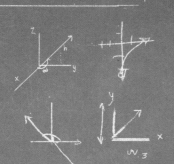

A	B
1	6
2	3
3	2
4	3/2

$A = \dfrac{K}{B}, \; K = 6$

$= x_0 + v_0 t + \tfrac{1}{2} at^2$

$= 3m, \; v_0 = 4 \tfrac{m}{s}, \; a = 2 \tfrac{m}{s^2},$

$t = 2s$

$x = 3\,m + \left(4 \tfrac{m}{s}\right)(2s)$

$+ \tfrac{1}{2} \left(2 \tfrac{m}{s^2}\right)(2s)^2$

$3m + 8m + 4m = \boxed{15\,m}$

Area Under
the curve

Approximate area $= \tfrac{2}{3} BH$

Area $= \displaystyle\int_a^b f(x)\, dx$

$6 - 4(-2 - x) = 5$

$6 + 8 + 4x = 5x$

$14 = x$

Circumference $= 2\pi r$

area $= \pi r^2$

$p = mv$

$m = 3kg \qquad v = 4 \tfrac{m}{s}$

$p = 12 \; \dfrac{kg \cdot m}{s}$

$\begin{bmatrix} 2 & 3 & 1 \\ 3 & -1 & -3 \\ 1 & 2 & 1 \end{bmatrix} \begin{bmatrix} x \\ y \\ z \end{bmatrix} = \begin{bmatrix} 7 \\ 4 \\ 1 \end{bmatrix}$

cube
rectangular prism

$F = ma$

$F = (3\,kg)(4 \tfrac{m}{s^2})$

$= 12\,N$

We love our Teacher!

MATHS CLASS is #1 !!

by
Katherine

For Katherine, her daughters,
and all who look to the stars
—H. B.

For Madeline, Audrey, and Sabrina —
all this and more
—D. P.

First published by Henry Holt and Company © Henry Holt is a registered trademark of Macmillan Publishing Group, LLC.

This edition published 2019 by Macmillan Children's Books
an imprint of Pan Macmillan
20 New Wharf Road, London N1 9RR
Associated companies throughout the world
www.panmacmillan.com

ISBN 978-1-5290-0559-2

1 3 5 7 9 8 6 4 2

A CIP catalogue record for this book is available from the British Library.

Design by Carol Ly
Printed and bound in China

Counting on KATHERINE

Illustrated by

HELAINE BECKER   **DOW PHUMIRUK**

MACMILLAN CHILDREN'S BOOKS

Katherine loved to count.

She counted the
steps to the road.

The steps up to church.

The number of dishes
and spoons she washed in
the bright white sink.

The only things she didn't count were the stars
in the sky. Only a fool, she thought, would try that!
Even so, the stars sparked her imagination.
What was out there?

Katherine yearned to know as much as she could about numbers, about the universe – about everything!

Katherine's boundless curiosity turned her into a star student. She was so bright, she skipped three whole school years. She catapulted right past her brother! (He wasn't too happy about that.)

6. 4(x-2) + 3(-x+4) = -2(x-3)
4x - 8 - 3x + 12 = -2x + 6
x + 4 = -2x + 6
3x = 2
x = 0.667
y = 1/3 x + 9
22.
10 3 10
total area = A + B + C
total area = 56 + 18 + 56 = 130
23. 6 - 4(-2 - x) = 5x
6 + 8 + 4x = 5x

By the time she turned ten,
Katherine was ready for high school.

But back then, America was
legally segregated by race.

Her town's high school didn't
admit black students – of any age.

Katherine burned with fury.
She wanted, more than anything,
to keep learning. There was still
so much to know.

"Count on me,"
Katherine's father told her.

WHITE SULPHUR SPRINGS,
WEST VIRGINIA

By working night and day, he earned enough money
to move the family to a town with a black high school.

INSTITUTE,
WEST VIRGINIA

Katherine loved high school. She was good at every subject, but maths was still her favorite. She dreamed of becoming a research mathematician, making discoveries about the number patterns that are the foundations of our universe.

In those days, though, there were no jobs as research mathematicians for women. Professions most available to them were teaching and nursing.

So Katherine became a primary school teacher. She liked her job. And she loved her students. But she never stopped dreaming about exploring numbers.

In the 1950s, the US government's National Advisory Committee on Aeronautics (NACA) hired thousands of new employees. It even started hiring black women — as mathematicians.

The Daily News

Hampton, Virginia

Evening Edition

More Women Join the Workforce

Mathematicians Needed at Langley Aeronautical Laboratory

Flight Test Data Analysis

air flow mid-engine

RESEARCH LAB

LANGLEY AERONAUTICAL LABORATORY
HAMPTON, VIRGINIA

Katherine heard about the mathematician jobs. Her heart raced with excitement — perhaps her dream could come true after all.

But when she applied for one of the positions, she was told they were already filled. Katherine had to wait a whole year until new spots opened up. Her patience paid off. She got the job.

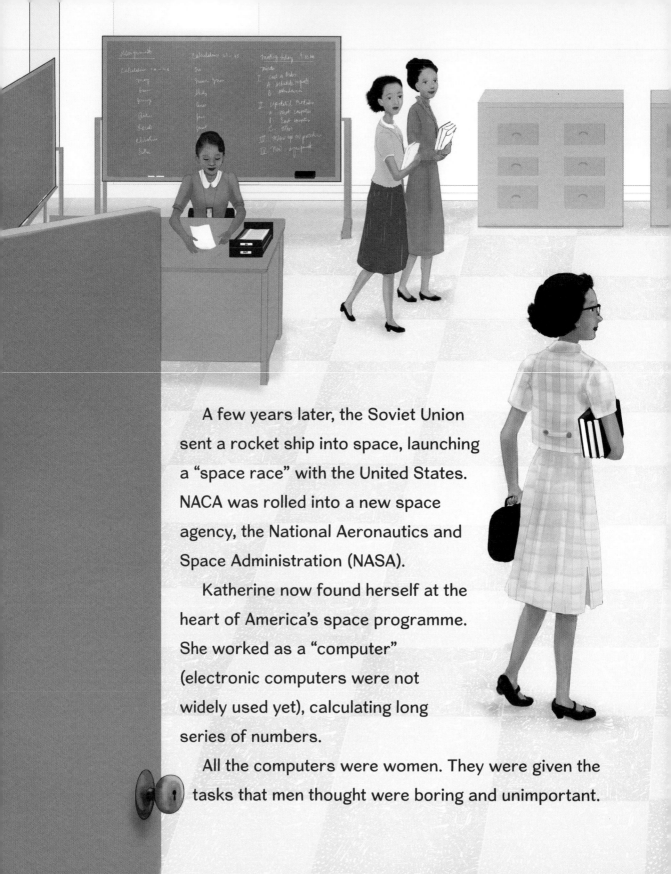

A few years later, the Soviet Union sent a rocket ship into space, launching a "space race" with the United States. NACA was rolled into a new space agency, the National Aeronautics and Space Administration (NASA).

Katherine now found herself at the heart of America's space programme. She worked as a "computer" (electronic computers were not widely used yet), calculating long series of numbers.

All the computers were women. They were given the tasks that men thought were boring and unimportant.

That didn't bother Katherine. She knew that without her contributions, a spaceship couldn't reach its destination, nor safely return to Earth.

Here's why:

Sending a rocket ship into space is like throwing a ball into the air. At first, the force of the throw sends the ball up, up, up! But as its energy runs out, the ball's path curves back towards the ground. Where it lands depends on what angle it was thrown and how high and how fast it flew.

Because maths is a kind of language, Katherine could ask those questions — how high would the rocket ship go and how fast would it travel? — using numbers. And numbers would provide the all-important answer: where would it land?

To find out, Katherine plotted the numbers she'd calculated on a graph. When she joined the points together, they formed a curved line.

At one end of that line was Earth at the time the rocket ship launched. At the other was where Earth would be when the ship landed.

Katherine's reputation for accuracy and strong leadership skills (she was known for asking plenty of questions!) got her promoted to Project Mercury, a new programme designed to send the first American astronauts into space.

Mercury's missions were going to be dangerous. So dangerous that even the project's star astronaut, John Glenn, refused to fly unless Katherine okayed the numbers.

"You can count on me," she said.

Glenn's spacecraft, *Friendship 7*, orbited Earth three times and returned home safely. Glenn became a national hero.

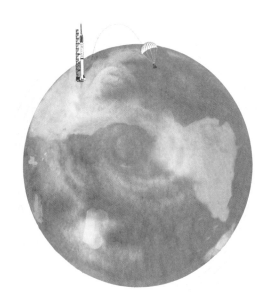

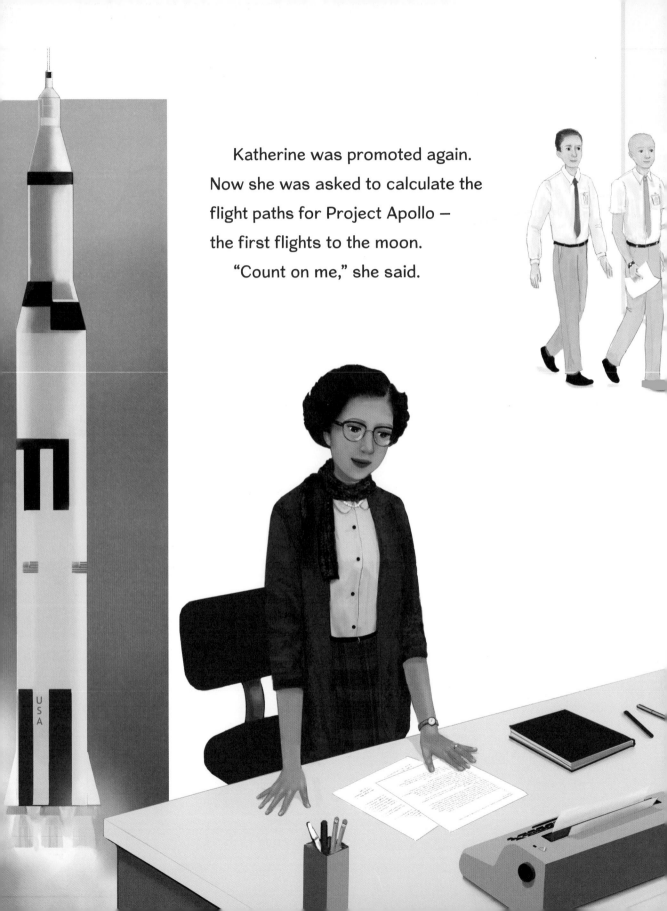

Katherine was promoted again.
Now she was asked to calculate the
flight paths for Project Apollo —
the first flights to the moon.
"Count on me," she said.

On July 20, 1969, the Apollo 11 astronauts walked on the moon. Their feat was celebrated around the world.

More triumphs followed. Apollo 12 rocketed to the moon in November 1969.

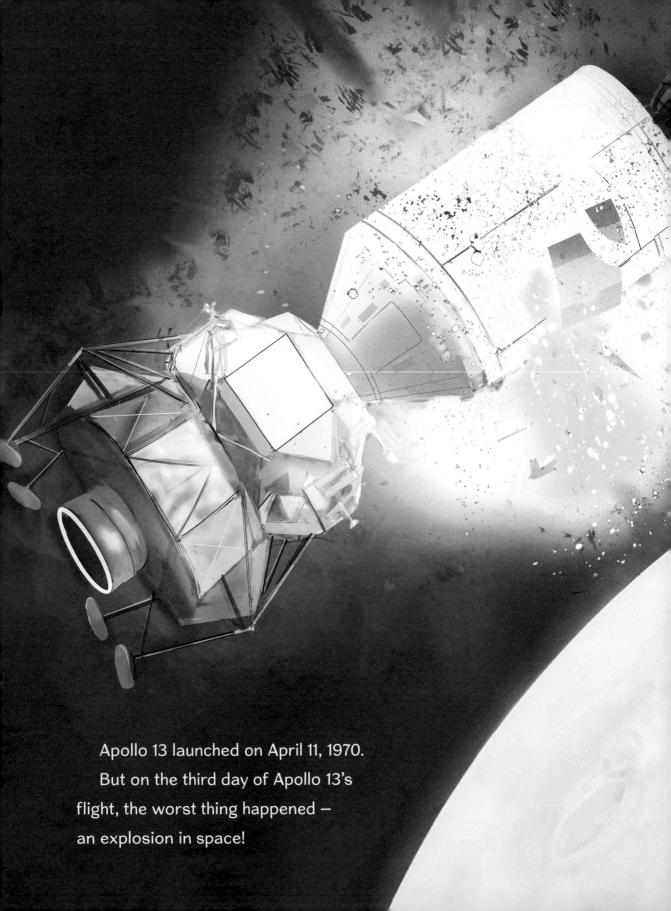

Apollo 13 launched on April 11, 1970.
But on the third day of Apollo 13's
flight, the worst thing happened —
an explosion in space!

Could the crippled spaceship make it to the moon?
And if it didn't, would it be able to get back home to Earth?
The three astronauts on board were in grave peril.

Commander Jim Lovell told mission
control: "Houston, we've had a problem."

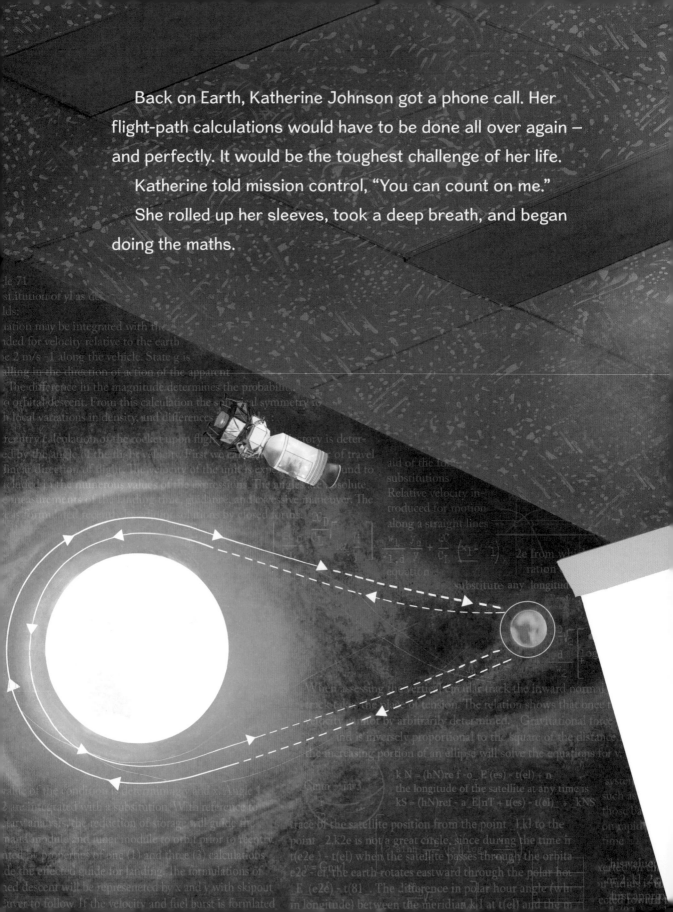

Back on Earth, Katherine Johnson got a phone call. Her flight-path calculations would have to be done all over again — and perfectly. It would be the toughest challenge of her life.

Katherine told mission control, "You can count on me."

She rolled up her sleeves, took a deep breath, and began doing the maths.

She worked hard and fast. A few hours later, Katherine's calculations were finished. The flight path to return home would take the ship around the far side of the moon. From there, the moon's gravity would act like a slingshot to zing the ship back to Earth. To get home, the crew of Apollo 13 would have to follow Katherine's course exactly by burning off fuel at precise intervals.

If the astronauts made a mistake, their ship would drift through space forever.

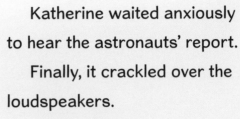

Katherine waited anxiously
to hear the astronauts' report.
Finally, it crackled over the
loudspeakers.
"WE'VE GOT IT!"
Apollo 13 was back on track.

Katherine Johnson had done it. She'd brought
Apollo 13 home.

She was no longer the kid who dreamed of what
lay beyond the stars. She was now a star herself.

$(x+3)^2 + (y+4)^2 = 27$

Jupiter

Mercury rocket

Mars

Apollo rocket

*K*atherine Johnson was born on August 26, 1918, in White Sulphur Springs, West Virginia. Her mother was a teacher. Katherine assumed she'd grow up to be a teacher, too.

From her youngest days, it was clear to everyone that Katherine was extremely bright. When she officially started school, she went straight into year three. Later, she skipped year six.

Katherine left high school at fourteen and West Virginia State College at eighteen. Her first job was teaching maths in Marion, Virginia. She loved helping her students learn, and encouraged them to learn from one another. "I had my students find a buddy and help each other."

In 1953, Katherine got a job as a "computer" at the Langley Aeronautical Laboratory for the National Advisory Committee for Aeronautics (later NASA). To counter ingrained sexism there, she had to develop more than maths skills. "We needed to be assertive as women in those days —assertive and aggressive." Still, Katherine was kept out of the research team's all-male briefings. "Eventually they got tired of answering all my questions and just let me in."

Spurred by competition with the Soviet Union, the United States ramped up its own space programme in 1958, and Katherine became an aerospace technologist when her team joined NASA. By the late 1960s, NASA estimates, more than 400,000 people were working on sending a man to the moon.

Katherine says, "The whole idea of going into space was new and daring. There were no textbooks — we had to write them. We wrote the first textbook by hand."

Katherine did her calculations on mechanical tabulating machines. By 1961, electronic computers were coming into wider use. But many people, including John Glenn, didn't trust the computer-generated numbers. "Call Katherine!" she remembers him saying. "If she says the number is right, I'll take it!"

Her role, however, always involved more than mere number

Earth

Moon

Capsule

Saturn

Uranus

crunching. It relied heavily on hunches. By letting her imagination run free, Katherine developed a key backup navigation system that used the stars as guideposts.

Katherine's contributions were crucial to America's space programme. She calculated the trajectory for Alan Shepard's first flight into space and devised the trajectories for space capsules and lunar landing modules. She co-authored twenty-six scientific papers, including a groundbreaking report on the theoretical underpinnings of space flight. Later in her career, she worked on the space shuttle and on a satellite project that searched the globe for underground minerals and other natural resources from space. In 2015, Katherine received the Presidential Medal of Freedom.

Despite her many achievements, Katherine never liked to take any credit. Her reason? "Because we always worked as a team," she says. "It was never just one person."

Neptune

SOURCES

Goodman, John L. *Apollo 13 Guidance, Navigation, and Control Challenges*. American Institute of Aeronautics and Astronautics Conference & Exposition. Pasadena, CA: Sept. 14–17, 2009.

Johnson, Katherine. Personal interview. Jan. 13, 2015.

The Makers Project, makers.com/katherine-g-johnson.

NASA. *Apollo 13 Air-to-Ground Voice Transcription*. Houston: April 1970.

NASA, nasa.gov. (See "Katherine Johnson: A Lifetime of STEM," Nov. 6, 2013; "From Computers to Leaders: Women at NASA Langley," March 27, 2014; "NASA Langley Research Center's Contributions to the Apollo Programme.")

NASA Cultural Resources (CRGIS), crgis.ndc.nasa.gov/historic/Katherine_ Johnson and crgis.ndc.nasa.gov/historic/Human_Computers.

Strickland, Zack. "Crew Brings Apollo 13 Mission to Safe Ending." *Aviation Week & Space Technology*, April 20, 1970: 14–18.

The Visionary Project, visionaryproject.org/johnsonkatherine/.

Warren, Wini. *Black Women Scientists in the United States*. Bloomington, IN: Indiana University Press, 1999.

WHROTV. "What Matters – Katherine Johnson: NASA Pioneer and 'Computer.'" Online video clip. YouTube. Published Feb. 25, 2011.

Sun

Mercury

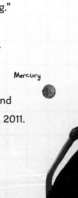

Friendship 7

Venus

Today's Date: August 26
Today's birthday: Katherine

Lesson 23 – 29

① Expand $(2x-4)^5$

$= (2x)^5 + 5(2x)^4(-4)^1$

$+ 10(2x)^3(-4)^2 + 10(2x)^2(-4)^3$

$+ 5(2x)^1(-4)^4 + (-4)^5$

$= 32x^5 - 320x^4 + 1280x^3$

$- 2560x^2 + 2560x - 1024$

② $x^2 + 6x + 9, x = 3$

$3^2 + 6(3) + 9$

$9 + 18 + 9 = 36$ ←

③
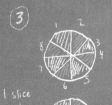

1 slice

Mrs. K brings 3 pies to the school picnic. Each pie is divided into 8 slices. There are 19 children from her class attending the picnic. How many slices are left if each child has one slice of pie?

$8 \times 3 = 24$ slices

$24 - 19 = 5$

Remainder = 5 slices.

④ $\sum_{k=0}^{3} (7-3k)$

$\sum_{k=0}^{3} (7-3k) = \underset{k=0}{(7-3(0))} +$

$\underset{k=1}{(7-3(1))} + \underset{k=2}{(7-3(2))} + \underset{k=3}{(7-3(3))}$

$= 7 + 4 + 1 - 2 = 10$

⑤ $-4(-2-x) = 5x+6$

$8 + 4x = 5x + 6$

$2 + 4x = 5x$

$2 = x$

⑥ $V = \frac{1}{3}\pi r^2 h$

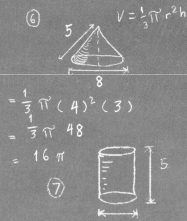
5

8

$= \frac{1}{3}\pi (4)^2 (3)$

$= \frac{1}{3}\pi \, 48$

$= 16\pi$

⑦
5

2

$V = \pi r^2 h$

$= \pi (1)(5)$

$= 5\pi$

⑧ $x^2 = 5x - 4$

$x^2 - 5x + 4 = 0$

$(x-1)(x-4) = 0$

$x = 1$ or 4

⑨ $(5x^2 + 4x$

$- (3x^2$

$= 5x^2 + 4x - 6$

$= (5x^2 - 3x^2$

$(4x + x)$

$= 2x^2 + 5x -$

Review

Example 1

$4x^6(3x^2 + x$

$4x^6(3x^2) + 4$

$-4x^6(1)$

$= 12x^8 + 4x^7 -$

Find the volume of an ice cream cone

$r = 2$

sphere

sphere $V = \frac{4}{3}\pi r$

cone

cone $V = \frac{1}{3}\pi r^2$